REVOLUTIONARY
T E X T I L E
D E S I G N

RUSSIA IN THE 1920s AND 1930s

I. YASINSKAYA

Introduced by JOHN E. BOWLT

A Studio Book
THE VIKING PRESS

N E W Y O R K

REVOLUTIONARY TEXTILE DESIGN

Copyright ©1983 by Idea Books
Introduction copyright ©1983 by Viking Penguin Inc.
Picture essay and research
Copyright ©1983 Evelina Schatz
Original Russian text and textile selection
Copyright ©1977 I. Yasinskaya
Translated from the Russian by Silvana de Vidovich
This English edition translated from the Italian
by Raymond Rosenthal

Published in 1983 by The Viking Press
(A Studio Book)
40 West 23rd Street
New York, N.Y. 10010

Published simultaneously in Canada by
Penguin Books Canada Limited

Library of Congress Cataloging in Publication Data

Yasinskaya, I.
   Revolutionary textile design.
   (A Studio book)
   1. Textile design — Soviet Union — History — 20th
century.   2. Constructivism (Art) — Soviet Union.
I. Title.
NK8856.A1S33   1983   667'.38'0947   82-21792
ISBN 0-670-59712-0
ISBN 0-670-59713-9 (paperback)

Book design by Anthony Mathews

Typesetting by Spingraf
Printed in Italy by G. Spinelli & C.

Illustration from *Heba*, 1922

Introduction

In April 1923 the artist Varvara Stepanova declared:
Fashion, which used to be the psychological reflection of everyday life, of customs and aesthetic taste, is now being replaced by a form of dress designed for use in various kinds of labor, for a particular activity in society. This form of dress can be shown *only during the process of work.* Outside of practical life it does not represent a self-sufficient value or a particular kind of "work of art."[1]

Stepanova was one of several Russian artists who became especially interested in textile and fashion design in the early 1920s, regarding it as a valuable discipline for the practical application of Constructivist ideas. Textile design, especially as formulated by Liubov Popova and Stepanova and, on a different level, by Sergei Burylin and Oskar Griun, became, along with stage design and porcelain and furniture design, one of the most exciting subjects for artistic experimentation in Moscow, Petrograd, and Ivanovo. Of course, this orientation was encouraged by the Constructivist sentiment that "Art . . . was artificially reheated by the hypocrisy of bourgeois culture and, finally, crashed against the mechanical world of our age. Death to art!"[2] Such ideas accelerated the move away from "pure" art to industrial design, a development that was associated particularly with the activities of the Institute of Artistic Culture in Moscow from 1921 on. It was there, in the fall of 1921, that artists such as Popova and Stepanova and their theoretical supporters, Boris Arvatov, Osip Brik, and Nikolai Tarabukin, resolved that industrial design was a creative medium well suited to the new proletarian society.

However, as with most theoretical pronouncements, the deed rather than the word was the beginning of Constructivism. It is important to remember that the notion of designing textiles and clothes for the new Soviet man and woman derived in part from the general demand to transform the outer appearance of Soviet Russia: it was argued that a new economic, social, and political structure must manifest itself in the actual environment, and Lenin's ambitious Plan of Monumental Propaganda, decreed in April 1918, may be regarded as an important stimulus to the Constructivist aspiration to redesign the whole of reality. Lenin demanded, for example, that "Monuments erected in honor of the tsars. . . be dismantled" and that artists produce "projects for monuments intended to commemorate the great days of the Russian Socialist Revolution."[3] The concrete results of Lenin's plan were far from satisfactory. The bureaucracy of Anatolii Lunacharsky's Commissariat for Enlightenment, which was responsible for implementation of the plan, worked clumsily, and many artists, not the least Vladimir Tatlin, viewed the scheme with grave misgivings. In any case, Lenin perceived "monumental propaganda" in terms of nineteenth-century statuary and neither he nor the public at large was pleased with the Cubo-Futurist structures that suddenly appeared on the streets and squares of Moscow and Petrograd.

Lenin's plan left much to be desired, but it did nurture, or coincide with, many other endeavors to superimpose symbols of the new regime on those of the old. Much has been written about the agit-decorations for buildings and transport produced in connection with the celebrations of May Day 1918 and of the first anniversaries of the Bolshevik Revolution in Moscow, Petrograd, and other cities.[4] Many artists, both avant-garde and moderate, helped to disguise the vestiges of tsardom with brightly colored, often geometric, designs carrying revolutionary images and captions. But this grand pageant seemed strangely out of place to a bewildered and indigent populace whose primary need was for food and clothing, not for avant-garde design. As the old lady in Alexander Blok's poem "The Twelve" (1918) puts it: "What's that poster for, that great big piece of material? It would make quite a few socks for our guys, and none of them has any clothes or shoes."[5]

It is tempting to interpret the positive response of leftist artists to agit-design in the first Revolutionary years as an indication of their staunch support of the new political ideals, but such a deduction is not entirely valid. Most of the Russian avant-garde, at least until 1917, were politically unaware and in any case enjoyed considerable artistic and civil freedom. True, they were regarded as buffoons or worse by the mercantile bourgeoisie, but they traveled freely in Russia and Europe, published numerous uncensored manifestoes, and organized shocking exhibitions and debates. What, then, did they expect to gain from the October Revolution? For some of the more practical artists such as Alexander Rodchenko and Vladimir Tatlin, the Revolution provided an opportunity to take art from private into public spaces — "to reconstruct not only objects, but also the whole domestic way of life";[6] for dreamers such as Kazimir Malevich the Revolution held a messianic, apocalyptic force that Russian philosophers and poets had long discussed; for a few, such as Pavel Filonov, the Revolution did, indeed, present a way to create a more democratic society; but for many, not least Vasilii Kandinsky, the Revolution was an inconvenience that interfered with the efficacy of their artistic lives. In other words, there was no single response, positive or negative, to the Revolutionary events so far as the avant-garde were concerned.

Furthermore, the world of design was not new to the Russian avant-garde. The fixtures for the famous Café Pittoresque in Moscow, often described as the first Soviet bohemian rendezvous, were designed by Rodchenko, Tatlin, Georgii Yakulov, and others in July and August of 1917, that is, without regard to the spirit of agit-art. In the field of textile and clothing design, Alexandra Exter, Malevich, Popova, Olga Rozanova, and others had all designed dresses, purses, cushions, and so forth *before* the Revolution, often with Suprematist motifs, and many of these were shown at the two Contemporary Decorative Art exhibitions in Moscow in 1916-1917. In fact, Natalia Goncharova designed "contemporary ladies' dresses" as early as 1913 for the St. Petersburg couturier Natalia Lamanova, who, in the 1920s, became a leading proponent of the new Soviet dress.

Of course, these were only tentative precedents to the brilliant Constructivist patterns produced by Popova and Stepanova, Exter and Lamanova, Rodchenko and Tatlin, in the early 1920s, and there is no question that the commitment of these artists to a new type of clothing was total. They argued that clothing must present the Soviet man and woman as part of an international community (hence the "anonymous," abstract motifs devoid of local, ethnic images), that it must connect them with industrial civilization (hence the geometric or mechanical motifs), and that it must symbolize emancipation and mobility (hence the frequent application of kinetic forms). Popova's and Stepanova's famous geometric textiles and their industrial or professional clothing (easily identifiable uniforms for sportsmen, actors, doctors, etc.), Tatlin's simple cut-out suit, Rodchenko's functional coverall, Burylin's and Griun's homage to engineering, were but a few of the many solutions to the problem of creating a new form of dress. For example, one group advocated nudity as the truly democratic costume and organized a series of "Evenings of the Denuded Body" in Moscow in 1922; the artist Yurii Annenkov liked the idea of throwaway paper clothing; Exter and Yakulov favored the high-fashion, bourgeois ensemble, maintaining that the proletarian woman also had the right to be "well dressed."

In spite of their claims to the contrary, the Constructivists were an elite and sophisticated group who really had little understanding of mass taste. Lamanova's dresses were modeled by Lilia Brik (Vladimir Mayakovsky's companion) and Elsa Triolet in Paris; Popova's dresses, ultimately, hardly differed from Sonia Delaunay's expensive garments for wealthy Parisiennes; and the idea of wearing no clothing or paper clothing in the Russian winter did not evoke enthusiasm. By 1924, and especially after the 1925 Exhibition of Decorative and Industrial Arts in Paris, where the close similarities between Soviet "Communist" and Western "capitalist" textile designs were immediately manifest, new definitions of Soviet textile design arose. A direct result was the rejection of the purely geometric motif in favor of symbolic images such as the hammer and sickle, cogwheels, and factories. These designs — illustrated here — acquired greater popularity than the purely abstract ones and were reproduced at mills all over the Soviet Union. They served at once as propaganda for the ongoing industrialization of the country, especially during the time of the First Five Year Plan, and as cheerful, dynamic designs that had immediate meaning for the workers and peasants.

This move toward a more narrative or thematic textile and clothing design paralleled the general orientation of Soviet culture in the late 1920s and 1930s to traditional, accessible styles. At first glance, these eulogies of technology, sports, transportation, and so on might seem to be more representative of the social and political aims of the young Soviet state, but if we stop to think, we might wonder how American tractors in bucolic rococo settings or Art Deco light bulbs looking like details from the Chrysler Building in New York City were any more Soviet or Communist than the Constructivist projects. Moreover, the meaning of the Red Army or Navy themes is lost as soon as the material is folded into a head scarf; and the noble symbology of the hammer and sickle is lost if you sit on it. The critic David Arkin lamented this in his survey of Soviet textiles in 1929: "An extreme abundance of very old designs and a breach between the designs and the form of dress are most characteristic of the entire artistic side of our textile industry."[7] But thanks precisely to this breach we can now disregard the original purpose of these textile designs and appreciate them for their color, their rhythm, their charming anachronism. In spite of Stepanova's impassioned words, we perceive them as "works of art."

John E. Bowlt

Notes

1. Varst (V. Stepanova): "Kostium segodniashnego dnia — prozodezhda" in *Lef*, Moscow, 1923, No. 2, April-May, p. 65.
2. Alexei Gan: *Konstruktivizm*, Tver, 1922. English translation in John E. Bowlt (ed.): *Russian Art of the Avant-Garde: Theory and Criticism 1902-1934*, New York: Viking, p. 221.
3. The decree was first published in *Izvestiia VTsIK*, Moscow, 1918, 14 April. reprinted in I. Grabar et al. (eds.): *Istoriia russkogo iskusstva*, Moscow: Academy of Sciences of the USSR, 1957, Vol. 11, p. 25.
4. The best source of information and illustrations on this subject is A. Galushkina et al. (eds.): *Agitatsionno-massovoe iskusstvo pervykh let Oktiabria*, Moscow: Iskusstvo, 1971.
5. A. Blok: "Dvenadtsat" (1918) in V. Orlov (ed.): *Alexandr Blok: Sochineniia v odnom tome*, Moscow-Leningrad: State Publishing House for Creative Literature, 1946, p. 257.
6. N. Tarabukin: *Ot molberta k mashine*, Moscow: Rabotnik prosveshcheniia, 1923, pp. 23-24.
7. D. Arkin: "Iskusstvo veshchi" in *Ezhegodnik literatury i iskusstva na 1929*, Moscow: Communist Academy, 1929, p. 450.

The first ten years that followed the October Revolution saw a prodigious development of the art of propaganda. The need to educate the people in the ideas and conquests of October gave rise to Lenin's plan for propaganda in the form of monumental decoration in streets and city squares, mass spectacles, and poetry composed on the occasion of the revolution's most significant anniversaries. Textiles also became a form of propaganda, together with political posters, graphics, and even porcelains.

The twenties and the beginning of the thirties represent a particularly interesting moment in the history of the Soviet textile industry. Cotton prints of this period, produced by mills in Moscow and its outskirts, in Leningrad, Slisselburg, Ivanovo and Serpuchovo, display a diversified panorama. On the one hand, there are Ivanovo's sateens and cotton prints with traditional pink and mauve bouquets against a red background or fabrics decorated with the "cucumber" design printed in the old style, and, on the other, fabrics with "informal" designs typical of Moscow's mills. Fabrics also imitated jacquard embroidery and designs, and more expensive fabrics, such as Karabanovo's gay cottons, were dyed with alizarin and used motifs from the old folk traditions and even more complicated designs. At the same time, fabrics were being produced of lightweight materials with almost no decoration.

Within this range, so varied in both quality and esthetic choice, fabrics

Petrograd, 1917

7

with propagandistic designs and on "new themes" — as they were then called — are particularly notable. The originality of these artistic studies and their innovative esthetic solutions make this sector of the textile industry especially interesting.

The rare, modest fabrics preserved in the Russian State Museum and the museums of Moscow, Zagorsk, Serpuchovo, and Ivanovo — those cottons, flannels, and sateens with decorations of the first Soviet symbols, the hammer and sickle, the red stars, the tools used in everyday and industrial work, compositions derived from folklore, and others reflecting the events of the postrevolutionary decade — are moving because of their immediate, direct response to questions of the moment. They spring from the desire of many artists to express, by means of fabrics, the atmosphere of mobilization common to that period, introducing into the daily life of the people an echo of revolutionary transformation, and in some way making fabric designs express the ideas of the revolution.

Decorative motifs offered, in various forms, themes which were popular during those years: "The Demonstration," "The Tractor," "Electrification," "The Struggle Against Illiteracy," "Pioneers," and "Factories." Many fabrics of this type have been preserved. Most of the designs reproduced in this volume come from the collection of the Russian State Museum in Leningrad. This collection was begun in 1931 through the efforts of I.V. Ginzburg, a specialist at the museum. It constituted the initial part of the Soviet Industrial Art Exhibit which was held in the museum at the end of 1931 and which was organized with the participation of the artists M.A. Grigoriev and N.M. Suetin. Its purpose was to present as com-

Rodchenko and Stepanova, about 1920

plete a picture as possible on both the productive and creative levels.

In this collection textiles coming from the mills in Ivanovo and Moscow predominated. Much less well known are the cloths produced in the Vera Slutskaya mills in Leningrad and in the Piotr Alexeyev mills in Slisselburg. The latter were destroyed during the great Civil War and now no longer exist. In fact, fabrics which testify to the activity of the Leningrad artists during the twenties and thirties are extremely rare.

The designs in the Soviet Textile Industry Exhibit that had opened in Moscow in 1923 were displayed — in 1931 — in a special section and belong only to the early twenties, years which coincide with a difficult period for the textile industry. Initially, in September 1920 the large plant set up at Ivanovo-Voznesensk was opened, and in October the Susnevkil plant. That same year the Treckgornaya mill in Moscow began operations again. At the beginning of 1921 the textile union counted 398 mills in the country, of which 286 were in operation. During the years of the economic crisis brought about by civil war and foreign intervention, the mills and factories — due to the scarcity of raw materials, skilled labor, and fuel — underwent a process not only of stagnation but actually of slow ruin. It appeared that hunger and the crisis would in the long run finish them off, yet despite these difficulties, towards the end of the twenties production was resumed in a number of mills — at Sui, Serpuchovo, Kinesma, Ivanovo, and Moscow.

Given these circumstances, it is clear that the artistic sector of production was not of a very high order. The textiles produced in that period, very small in quantity when compared to the needs of a population living through the hardships of the civil war, were quite simple, with printed decorations based on old patterns that required only a very elementary manufacturing process. The textile industry attained a more stable footing in 1923. As a consequence, the textile mills were able to participate in the Pan-Russian Artistic Products Exhibit, which opened in March 1923, and the Pan-Russian Agricultural Exhibit, where a special textile pavilion was set up. "This exhibit," a weavers' newspaper commented, "is the first in the world which does not have commercial and advertising aims. Our exhibit provides material for thought and study."

Participants in the Pan-Russian Exhibition included such well-known artists as V. Muchina and A. Exter, contributors in those days to *Fashion Atelier*. This magazine, founded in Moscow at the beginning of 1923, had as its goal the creation of a new kind of modern dress which would correspond to the exigencies of the new forms of Soviet life. "The rhythm of modern life," Exter wrote, "demands a minimum loss of time and energy. To present-day fashions which change according to the whims of the merchants, we must counterpose a way of dressing that is functional and beautiful in its simplicity . . ." (T. Strizenova, in *Decorative Art in the USSR*, 1967, no. 1, p. 31). That same year *Fashion Atelier* began publishing an illustrated magazine whose contributors, together with

Exter and Muchina, included the artists S. Cechonin, B. Kustodiev, K. Juon, and K. Petrov-Vodkin. In this magazine there was no talk of a new kind of cloth, yet it goes without saying that a new type of dress was unthinkable without a new type of textile decoration. In fact, the publication of *Fashion Atelier* did not get beyond its first number. Yet this one issue showed how already at the beginning of the twenties, when the So-

Rodchenko, "Champions, England and France," watercolor and ink, 1919

viet textile industry was barely overcoming the crisis, the people involved were concerned with the esthetic nature of their products. This is also shown in an article that appeared at the beginning of 1923 in *Pravda*, urging artists to deal with industrial problems. The first artists to respond to this appeal were L. Popova, V. Stepanova, A. Rodchenko, and A. Exter, who sent their sketches to the first mill which made cotton prints in Moscow. They were young artists, pioneers, enthusiastic about industrial art, fascinated by the problems of artistic construction, and impelled by the romantic dream of making art a part of the people's daily life.

"Cotton cloth is a product of artistic culture just as much as a painting; there is no reason to distinguish one from the other," the art critic J. Tugencholyed wrote. "In the textile field, instead of the previous old imitations of foreign models, we have new fabric designs created by young artists under the guidance of L. Popova, designs in which for the first time the research of artists on the Left has been applied to the industry; they reflect all the intense dynamic of life" (E. Murina in *Decorative Art in the USSR*, 1967, no. 8, p. 24). They were easy to produce, modern in style, and printed in large quantities. F. Roginskaya, the art historian, described these textile designs executed by the Constructivists as "the first

The group Unisov, Vitebsk, 1920: Ermolaeva, Malevich, Tchichimik, El Lissitzky

An agit-prop group painting a railroad car

Soviet fashion" (F. Roginskaya, *Soviet Textile Industry*, 1930, p. 36).

Alongside the work of the Constructivists, there were other schools of textile design. There were fabrics with subjects whose ornamental design recalled the surrounding world. The very titles of these subjects — "October," "Collectivization," "Flying Squads," "The Factory," "Industry," "Building Construction" — prove that they were directly connected with daily life. These designs, produced by many mills and sold in the most remote corners of the Soviet Republic, played an important role in propaganda and in support of socialist ideas. They celebrated the first Five-Year Plan, the Oriental peoples' awakening to a new way of life, and the struggle against illiteracy. In these designs one can feel the pulse of the times, the intense activity of a country transformed by the October Revolution. Unlike the textile designs of the Constructivists, which critics described as "abstract" or "geometric," these works were called "thematic" or "propaganda" patterns. When they were put on the market or shown at exhibits, they provoked heated debates. Articles by O. Brik, N. Poluektovaya, F. Roginskaya, and others published in the periodical press remind us of the lively polemic atmosphere of those years. Between 1927 and 1931 "thematic" designs predominated. They were created and popularized by such textile artists as L. Silich, O. Fedoseyeva, D. Preobrazhenskaya, M. Chvostenko, F. Antonova, M. Nazarevskaya, and L. Raitsev, all graduates of VCHUTEIN (Textile Faculty of the Institute of Arts and Industrial Design), and by old local designers such as S. Burylin and V. Maslov, experts in production. The Textile Section of the Youth Union in the Association of Artists of the Revolution, whose founders were the artists M. Nazarevskaya, L. Raitsev, and F. Roginskaya, played an active part in the wide-scale distribution of these new designs.

Thematic designs varied greatly. Some reproduced mechanically the old compositions of the past, while others proposed new motifs. One of the most characteristic was the sateen "Tractor," widely distributed in those times, devised by the Ivanovo artist V. Maslov, the first example of this new kind of design. The theme, which symbolized the life of a Soviet village, was very popular in those years and was used in many variations. In Maslov's design, against a light blue-gray background, large figurative factory trademarks are framed by bunches of berries, fruits, and dark green leaves. In the free spaces are scenes of agricultural work. A

Rodchenko, illustration from the magazine *Lef*

type of decorative composition which goes back to the French silks of the seventeenth and eighteenth centuries could also be seen among the national textiles. Maslov introduced into this old compositional scheme a more up-to-date theme, combining narrative design with elementary symbology, fused together by graphic style and a luminous color range, according to the tradition of the Ivanovo mills. The richness of

Banners on the old Marinsky Palace (above) and the panel "Birth of the New World" (below)

14

color in these cloths, its difficulty of execution, which requires a series of complicated printing procedures, make it clearly superior to other cloths produced during those years, which were made with only one or two rollers. Probably the fabric was executed as a design to be exhibited; in fact, at the Moscow Soviet Textile Industry exhibit, which opened in 1928, it was presented as a prototype for possible textile production.

Some of the cloth produced in the large mill at Ivanovo-Voznesensk is similar in both subject and composition to the "Tractor" fabric. It does not have a particular name. The fact that the idea of a narrative pattern, the composition, and the entire design are treated in a similar fashion leads one to think that its creator may be Maslov. Unfortunately, our information about this artist is meager. We know that he worked in the mill at Teikov, but his designs apparently were not printed in Teikov alone.

In the spirit of the traditional Ivanovo fabrics, unknown artists produced a series of dress materials printed with bright-color roses surrounded by airplanes that remind us of the traditional *millefleurs*. Despite their conventionality, these works are distinguished by their highly decorative and festive air, characteristic of traditional Russian decoration.

Once again these examples indicate the difficult conditions under which textile artists of the twenties functioned in their search for new

Varvara Stepanova (second from right) with students from the Vchutemas, about 1920

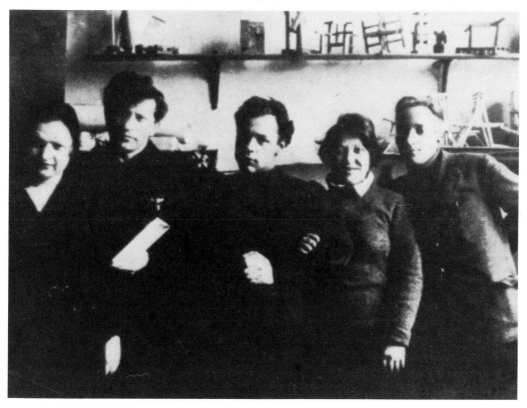

Rodchenko, drawings for an overall (1921), teapot (1922), and lamp (1929)

images of everyday life. Some of these works show precise and original artistic solutions. This is the case of the sateens with decorations on the theme "Work to Transform the Countryside." In these instances, as in the tractor fabric, traditional criteria typical of the old brocades are used. Nevertheless, here the theme is used only as a pretext for compositions that are in themselves much more interesting and resolved at a level of abstraction and stylization.

In one case, the decoration inserted on broad stripes coincides with the weft of the cloth, which acts as a decorative background element. This relationship and the compositional stylization of the details — tractors, people, sheaves of wheat — render the whole barely perceptible from a distance. The composition acquires a particularly intense energy from the contrast of the groupings, and from the rhythmical succession of colors, orange, blue, and pink. The author is unknown, although the oldest artists of the Ivanovo mill tend to think that this is the work of Sergei Petrovich Burylin, a well-known designer, the author of many textile designs.

Burylin (1876 - 1942), together with Popova and Stepanova, should be regarded as one of the pioneers of Soviet textile art. Among the Ivanovo textile artists whose work has made the fabrics of this city famous, he occupies an important place as an innovator of textile design. "His work belongs to the great and original school of Ivanovo fabrics" — so his colleague S. Loginov described Burylin (in *Workers World*, 1967). Burylin's compositional designs express a special virtuosity. They are elegant classical etchings against a black background, or blue caps with red stars combined harmoniously with images of fish and fishermen's nets, or light cotton prints for dresses with decorations of mechanical gears or stacks of wheat. Burylin's fabrics with minute designs in the form of ears of wheat, five-pointed stars, and hammers and sickles were shown at the Universal Exposition in Paris in 1925 and won the gold medal. The son of an illustrator, Burylin had no professional artistic education, yet he knew perfectly all the coloring and composition criteria required by factory production. His school was the factory. Observing the variety of his fabrics, one notices that the new themes, although not always carried out successfully, did not daunt the artist. His work testifies to the fact that uppermost in the minds of all these artists was the need to create a new textile style.

In one series of fabrics some artists attempted to portray the conquests of the first Five-Year Plan, the new style of Soviet life, and the dynamic rhythm and beauty of industrial processes. This series, whose composition represented stylized details of industrial elements, was described as "Designs of Production". A typical example is the fabric designed by the artist R. Matveyeva of the great Ivanovo-Voznesensk plant. It is a dress fabric whose compositional elements are based on the rhythmic repetition of the objects tied to production: sickle, hammer, black outlines of gear wheels. The details, felicitously harmonized with a series of colors, meet the specific requirements of textile decoration.

The floral decoration typical of foreign bourgeois taste in the thirties was supplanted by thematic designs, industrial motifs, or related patterns which describe events that had become recurrent after the October Revolution. Quite common are textiles on themes such as "Electrifi-

Porcelain

cation," "Building," and "The Work and Customs of Oriental Peoples." This last theme especially was developed in a series of variations preserving the stylistic elements of Oriental textiles. A further development is recorded in 1930, when many artists who had graduated from VCHUTEIN, such as E. Lapsinaya and O. Fedoseyeva, who worked on the themes of "Aviation" and "Tractors," joined the Ivanovo mills. With very simple means — for example, the well-known dotted design with a red outline produced with a single roller — the artist was able to transform a simple functional cloth into a work of art.

An interesting series of thematic designs is tied to the name of O. Bogoslovskaya, graduated in 1929 from the Artistic Industrial Institute, who worked at first in the Sosnev mill and later in the mill in Ivanovo which bears the name of the worker F. Zinoviev. Her "Electrification" design on Indian cloth is particularly original and represents a successful combination of the qualities of the cloth with elements of novelty. The proportions of the design of the light bulb, with rays of light, and the color combine in a free association with a floral decoration, a recurrent characteristic of this artist. In watercolor sketches donated by the artist to the Russian Museum in 1972, her great love of color is evident and the painterly principle typical also of her later work predominates.

Cup and saucer

A special contribution to fabric design was made at the end of the twenties by O.P. Griun, an artist in the mill at Treckgornaya and one of the teachers at VCHUTEIN. His designs are extremely personal and most unusual. Usually Griun included in the composition various details connected with textile production, such as spools and other instruments. The choice of color, the precise proportions of the design, the manner in which it was deployed across the surface, point to an artist of great talent. He had particular success with a fabric painted with Soviet emblems and a representation of the world surrounded by the rays of the sun. The arrangement of these elements, the precision of the design, perceptible even at a distance, and the color contrasts evoked considerable emotional response. The romantic enthusiasm of the basic idea, its symbolic meaning, show us the feeling that infused those ten post-revolutionary years.

Preobrazhenskaya's works for the Ivanovo and Moscow mills offer further examples of fresh originality. They are fabrics on the subjects of "Swimmers" and "The Eighth of March," among others. Her flannel print of "Swimmers" is outstanding because of the skill with which the theme is stylized by the repetition of agile silhouettes. The "Eighth of March" design has a wide gamut of pink tones which in the distribution of the de-

Nina Kogan, gouache, about 1930

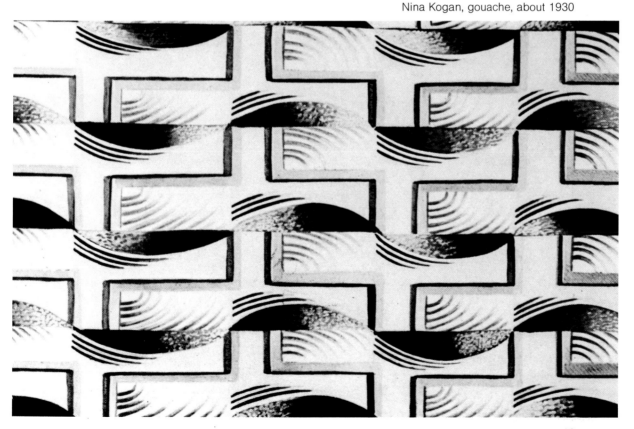

Varvara Stepanova, photograph by Rodchenko, about 1925

sign recalls the traditional curtains that were once popular among the peasants. However, the dynamic solution of the compositions and the festive quality of the subject make this fabric very "modern" for those years.

One of the most talented graduates of the VCHUTEIN was L. Silich, whose diploma design, a dress fabric called "The Reaper" or "The Peasant," executed according to the old piquet technique (extremely thin white lines on a colored background) is striking because of its elegant simplicity and its concise and delicate stylization. The repetition of women holding sheaves of wheat imparts a flowing rhythm to the decoration.

Artists of this period had to be concerned not only with problems of an esthetic order but also with creating a design whose elements of novelty could be reproduced under conditions of mass production. Kerchiefs such as "Airplanes" and "Collectivization," by Fedoseyeva, and "The Rye" by Bobysev, belong to the series executed on rollers. Limited production possibilities and the great demand for fabrics compelled the artists to economize as much as possible on artistic means. This explains in part the vast spread of designs executed on a single roller during the years 1927 - 1929, in which the background color of the material is an integrating part of the design. Within the limitations of a single color - red, black, dark blue - together with the basic background, the artists were able to achieve an exceptional decorative expressiveness. It is enough to cite such prints as Burylin's "Tractor," Matveyeva's "Water Sports," Preobrazhenskaya's "Transportation," and Raitsev's "Demonstration."

Different in color, execution, number of rollers used, and variety of ornamental elements are the fabrics produced on commission for specific celebrations. The design of the fabric executed in 1933 by Raitsev, "Mechanization of the Red Army," celebrating the fifteenth anniversary of the Red Army, has a particularly solemn and monumental aspect, just as the cotton print by P. Leonov with images of factories, airplanes, and sunbeams is brilliantly festive. The problems and exigencies of textile design during the period under examination are many and diverse. We have seen certain cases where the subject represented for the artist a kind of canvas on which to elaborate an ornamental design which, although recalling the chosen theme by association, did not illustrate it — in other words, cases in which the theme is subordinate to the specificity of the textile design. In others, however, the narrative principle was predominant and the fabric became a way of illustrating a particular subject. In the twenties and thirties there were many examples of the latter, as is shown in the case of Maslov, creator of the famous "Tractor" fabric and another cotton print on the theme of "Collectivization." Maslov not only uses several rollers but also adopts the technique of fading, which imitates a painter's brush strokes, perspective, and volume, and includes in

ТАРЕЛКИН

Varvara Stepanova, costumes, 1923

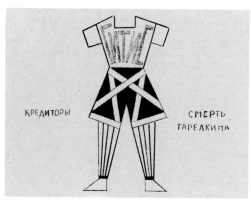

КРЕДИТОРЫ
СМЕРТЬ ТАРЕЛКИНА

Liubov Popova, textile design (left and right), dress design (center), 1923-24

the design the text, "Society of Rural Consumption." The whole, together with the narrative subject of the scenes, gives one the impression of being confronted by a work done on an easel. The incompatibility between the nature of the cloth and these decorative methods was even more evident when the design was meant for a dress fabric. Examples of such contrast between the artist's idea and the final use of a particular cloth are numerous, and once again prove how complex was the path chosen by the artists in their search for an ornamental design in harmony with the times. Their desire to be as persuasive as possible in the choice of new subjects often forced them to scale down their ideas and to use on fabrics esthetic elements that were typical of the poster, easel painting, and publishing graphics.

The fabrics produced during the twenties present us with a complex if

Varvara Stepanova and Liubov Popova, textile designs

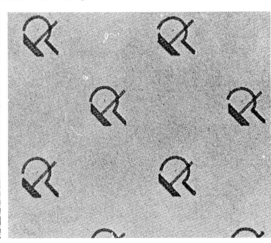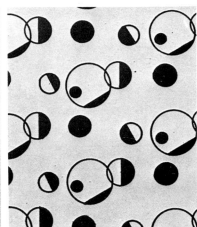

not contradictory panorama. It was a passing moment and, as was shown by the subsequent development of textile design, it was unrepeatable from the historic point of view. During the thirties there arose a renewed interest in floral decoration, which responded to new esthetic problems. Just as important are the works of those artists who strove to create a new Soviet style in textiles, a style which, without any kinship to others, would represent the characteristic traits of the epoch. These works offer us the possibility of perceiving directly the unique atmosphere of those years. Thus they preserve their fascination and their value not only for scholars of the subject, but also for those artists who are active in this field today.

I. Yasinskaya

Alexandra Exter, 1923

SOSNEV AMALGAMATED MILLS

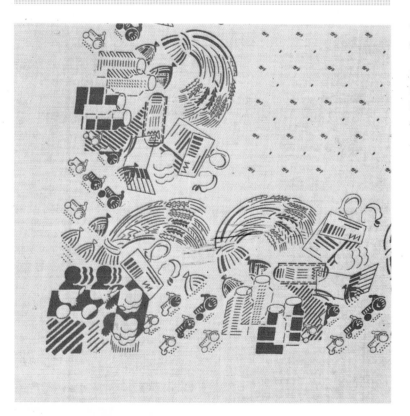

"The Collectivization"
Cotton print
1928-1930s
Fragment of a kerchief
Designed by O. Fedoseyeva
Russian Museum, Leningrad
Acquired in 1931.

facing page:
Cotton print
Late 1920s-early 1930s
Designer unknown
The I. Yasinskaya Collection,
Leningrad.

"Aquatic Sports"
Cotton print
1928-1930s
Designed by E. Lapshina
Russian Museum, Leningrad
Acquired in 1931.

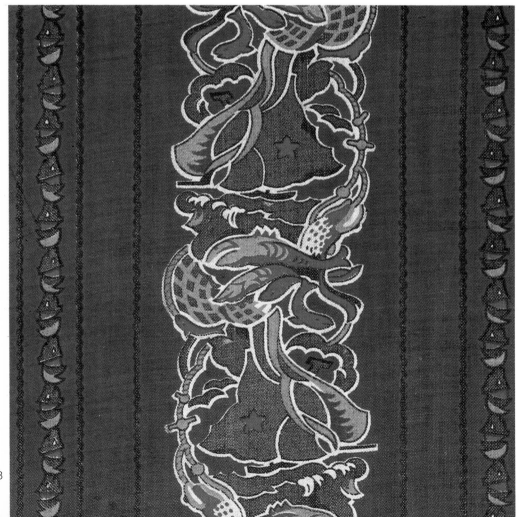

Cotton print
Late 1920s-early 1930s
Designed by S. Burylin (?)
The I. Yasinskaya Collection,
Leningrad.

"Waste Utilization"
Cotton print
Late 1920s-early 1930s
Designer unknown
Russian Museum, Leningrad
Acquired in 1931.

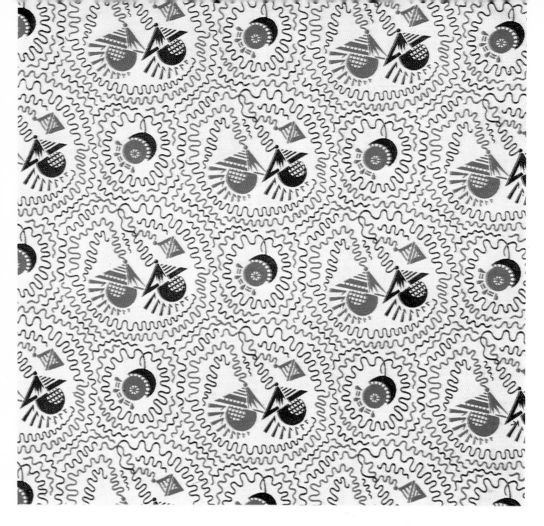

"Electric Bulbs"
Cotton print
1928-1930s
Designed by E. Lapshina
Russian Museum, Leningrad
Acquired in 1931.

"The Turkestan-Siberia Railroad"
Cotton print for the
Soviet Republics of Central Asia
1927-1930
Designer unknown
Russian Museum, Leningrad.

"Construction Site"
Cotton print
1920-1930
Designed by O. Bogoslovskaya (?)
Russian Museum, Leningrad
Acquired in 1931.

Cotton print
For the Soviet Republics of
Central Asia
Late 1920s-early 1930s
Designer unknown
Russian Museum, Leningrad
Acquired in 1931.

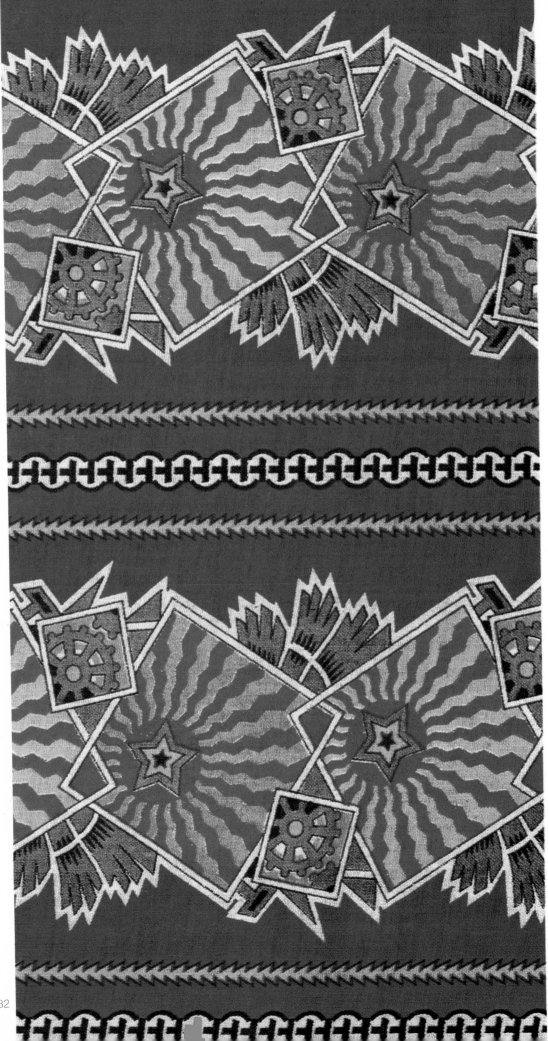

Cotton print
Late 1920s-early 1930s
Designed by S. Burylin (?)
The I. Yasinskaya Collection,
Leningrad.

facing page:
"Electric Bulbs"
Cotton print for the Soviet
Republics of Central Asia
1928-1930s
Designed by S. Strusevich
Russian Museum, Leningrad
Acquired in 1931.

32

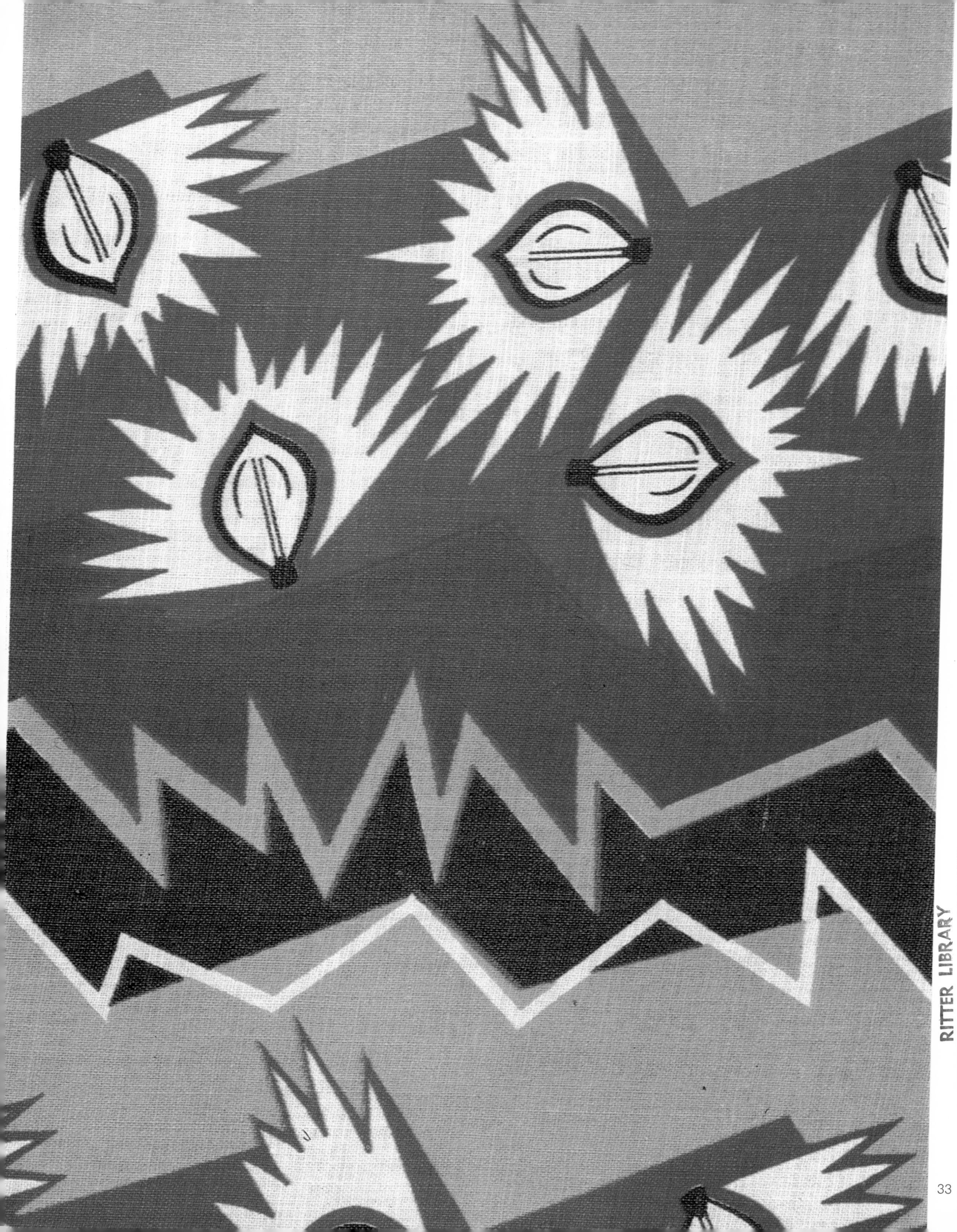

Cotton print
Late 1920s-early 1930s
Designed by S. Burylin (?)
The I. Yasinskaya Collection,
Leningrad.

Cotton print
Late 1920s-early 1930s
Designer unknown
The I. Yasinskaya Collection,
Leningrad.

"Fifteenth Anniversary
of the USSR"
Cotton print
Early 1930s
Designed by O. Bogoslovskaya (?)
The I. Yasinskaya Collection,
Leningrad.

"Electrification"
Cotton print
Early 1930s
Designed by O. Bogoslovskaya
The I. Yasinskaya Collection,
Leningrad.

Cotton print
Industrial motif
Late 1920s-early 1930s
Designed by S. Burylin (?)
The I. Yasinskaya Collection,
Leningrad.

IVANOVO - VOZNESENSK MILLS

"Skaters"
Flannel
Late 1920s-early 1930s
Designed by D. Preobrazhenskaya
Russian Museum, Leningrad
Acquired in 1931.

facing page:
Cotton print
1924-early 1930s
Designer unknown
Russian Museum, Leningrad
Acquired in 1931.

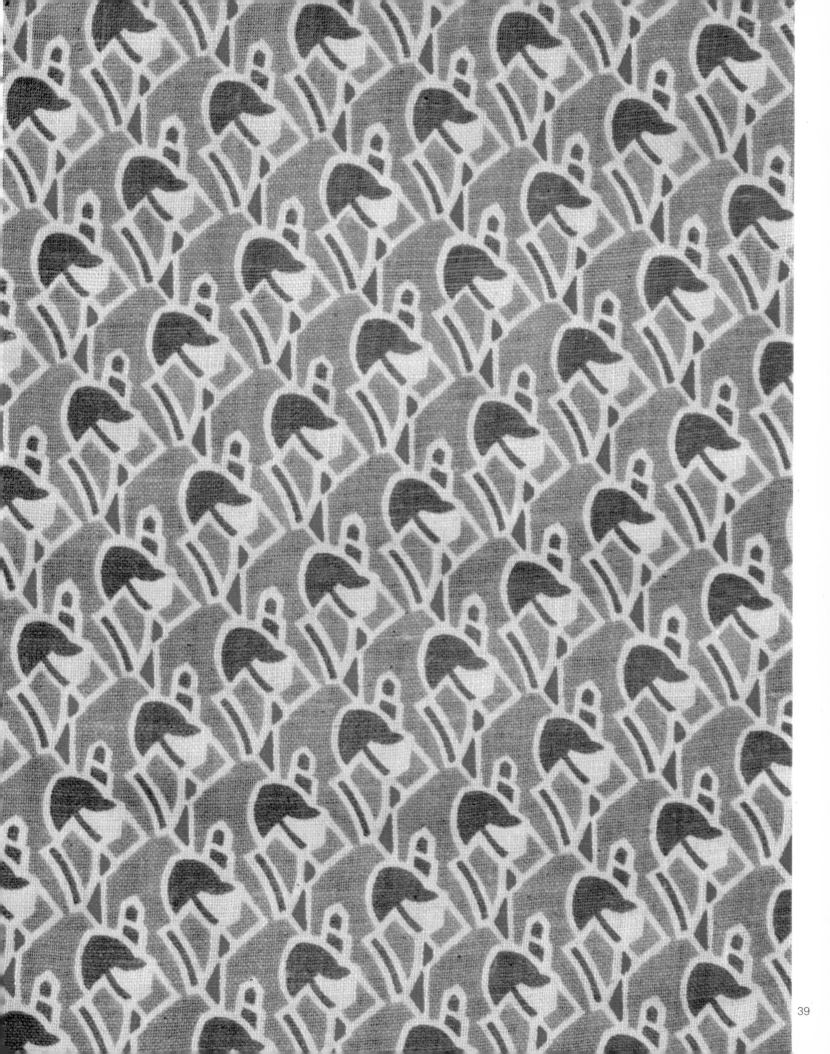

"Transport"
Cotton print
1927
Designed by D. Preobrazhenskaya
Russian Museum, Leningrad
Acquired in 1931.

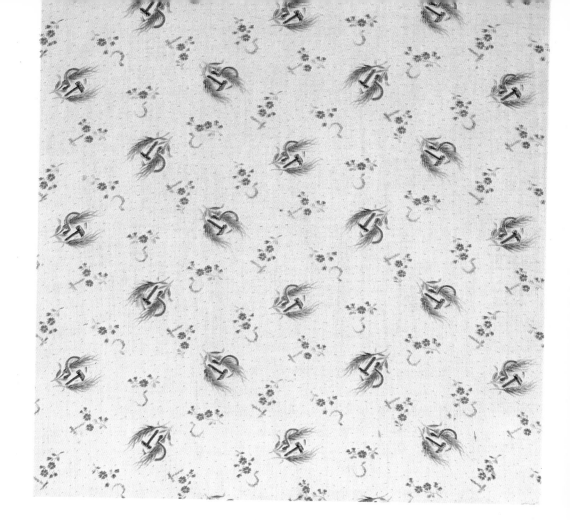

Cotton print
1924-1925
Designed by S. Burylin
Russian Museum, Leningrad
Acquired in 1931.

Cotton print
1924-1925
Designed by S. Burylin
Russian Museum, Leningrad
Acquired in 1931.

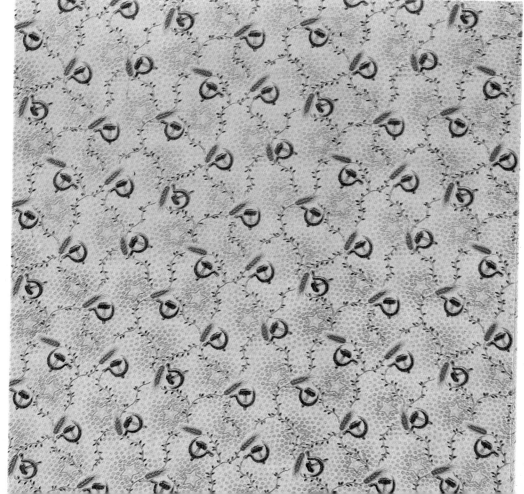

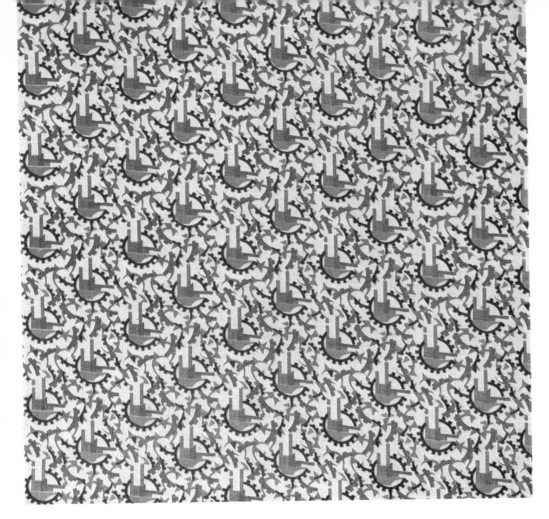

"Industry"
Cotton print
1929
Designed by R. Matveyeva
Russian Museum, Leningrad
Acquired in 1931.

Cotton print
1927
Designed by R. Matveyeva
Russian Museum, Leningrad
Acquired in 1931.

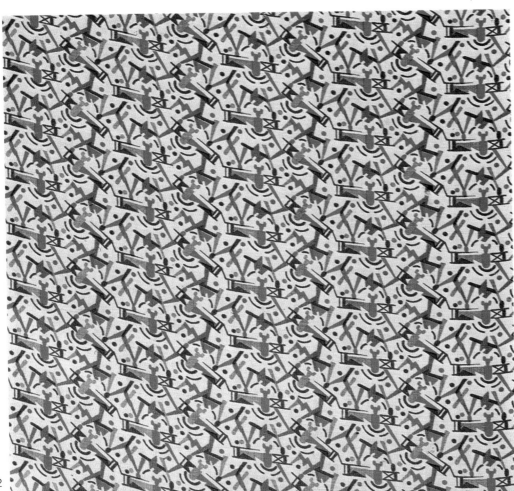

Crepe
1927
Designed by S. Burylin
Russian Museum, Leningrad
Acquired in 1931.

"Industry"
Crepe
1930
Designed by S. Burylin
Russian Museum, Leningrad
Acquired in 1931.

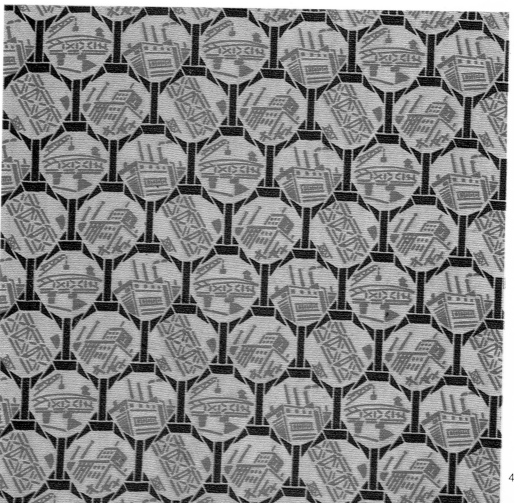

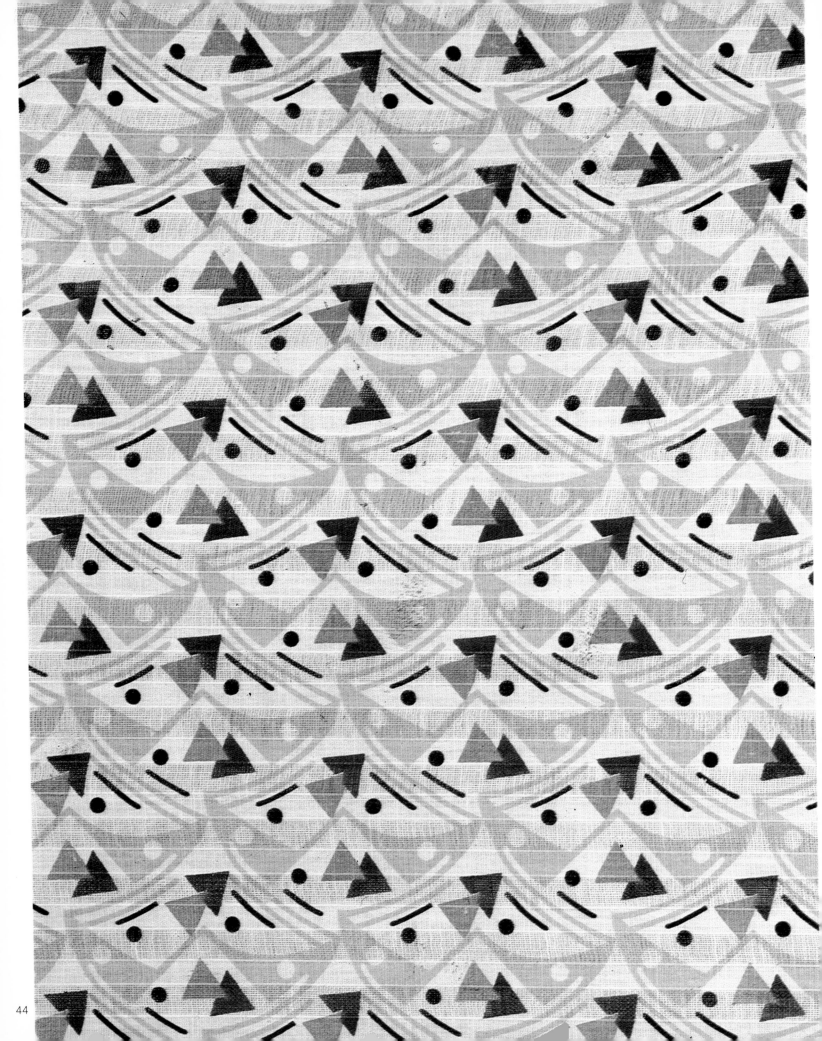

44

"Industry"
Cotton print
1930
Designed by D. Preobrazhenskaya
Russian Museum, Leningrad
Acquired in 1931.

facing page:
Armure
1927
Designed by A. Medvedev
Russian Museum, Leningrad
Acquired in 1931.

"Factory"
Cotton print
1927
Designed by S. Burylin
Russian Museum, Leningrad
Acquired in 1931.

Decorative cotton print
1927
Designed by P. Leonov
Russian Museum, Leningrad
Acquired in 1931.

facing page:
Armure
1927
Designed by S. Burylin
Russian Museum, Leningrad
Acquired in 1931.

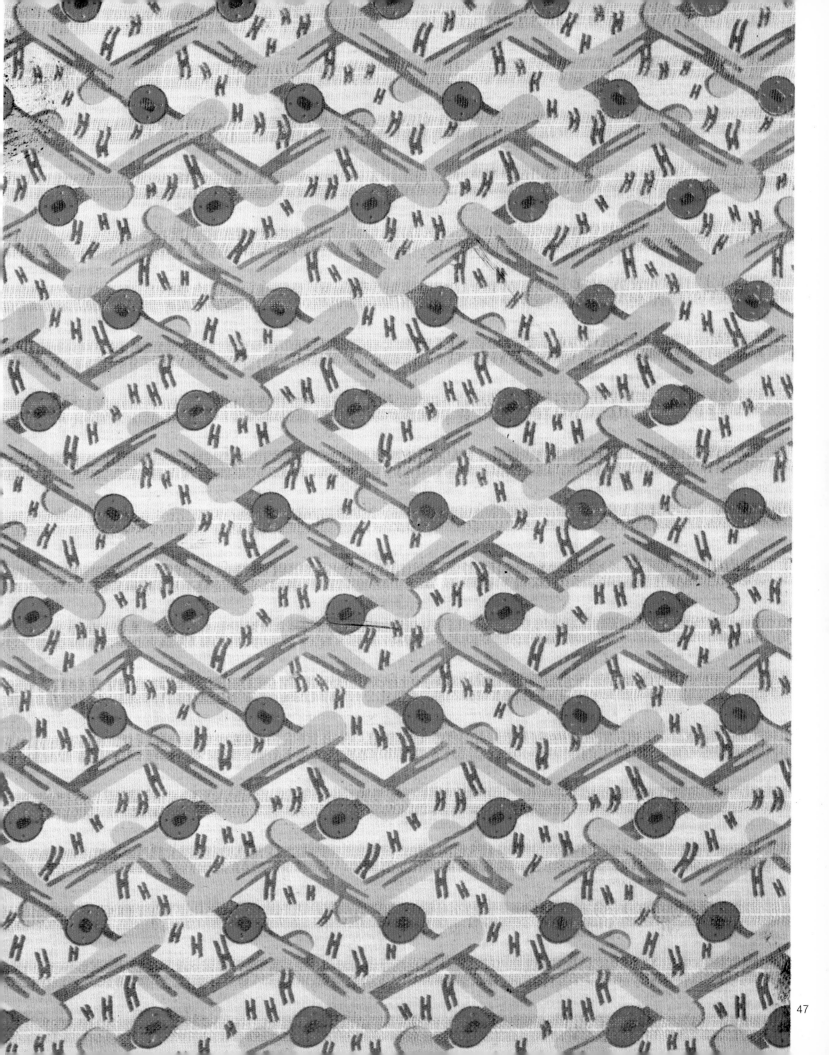

47

"Tractor"
Cotton print
1930
Designed by S. Burylin
Russian Museum, Leningrad
Acquired in 1931.

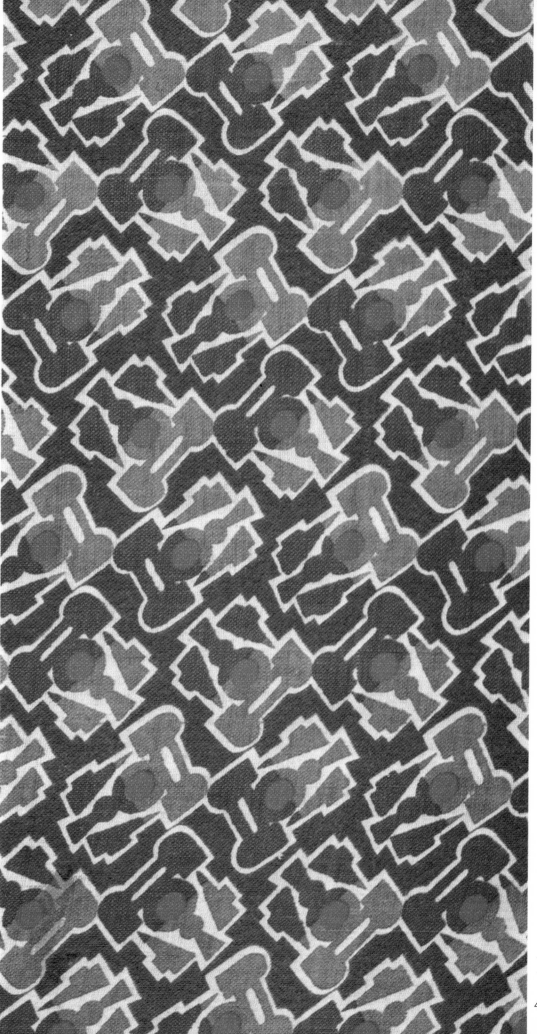

"Steam engine"
1927-1930
Designed by P. Nechvalenko
Russian Museum, Leningrad
Acquired in 1931.

49

"The Collectivization"
Cotton print
Late 1920s
Designed by V. Maslov (?)
The I. Yasinskaya Collection,
Leningrad.

"Tractor"
Sateen
Late 1920s
Designed by V. Maslov
Russian Museum, Leningrad
Acquired in 1931.

Armure
1927
Designed by S. Burylin
Russian Museum, Leningrad
Acquired in 1931.

"TREKHGORNAYA MANUFAKTURA" MILL

"Mechanization of the Red Army
Sateen
1933
Designed by L. Raitser
The V. Mukhina Higher School of
Art and Design, Leningrad.

facing page:
"Young Pioneers"
Serge
Late 1920s-early 1930s
Designed by O. Griun
Russian Museum, Leningrad
Acquired in 1931.

Cotton print
Late 1920s-early 1930s
Designer unknown
The I. Yasinskaya Collection,
Leningrad.

"Aquatic Sports"
Flannel
Late 1920s-early 1930s
Designed by D. Preobrazhenskaya
Russian Museum, Leningrad
Acquired in 1931.

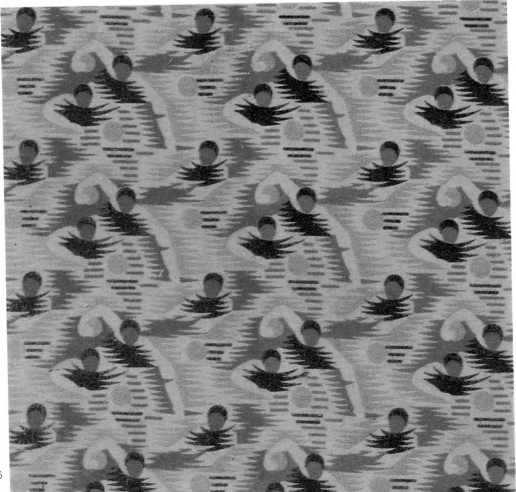

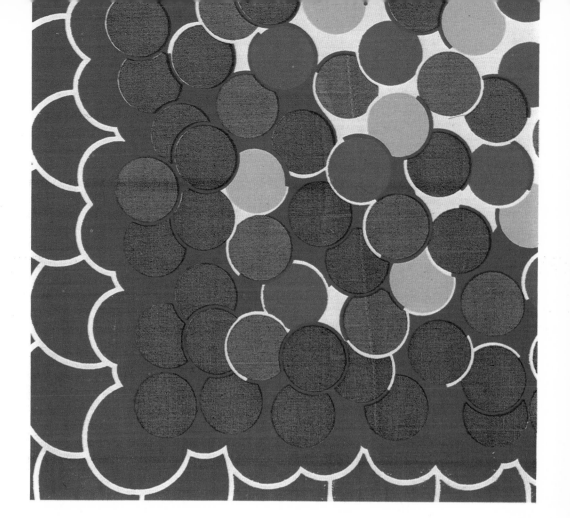

Cotton print
Late 1920s-early 1930s
Fragment of a kerchief
Designer unknown
Russian Museum, Leningrad
Acquired in 1931.

"Demonstration"
Cotton print
1929
Designed by L. Raitser
Russian Museum, Leningrad
Acquired in 1931.

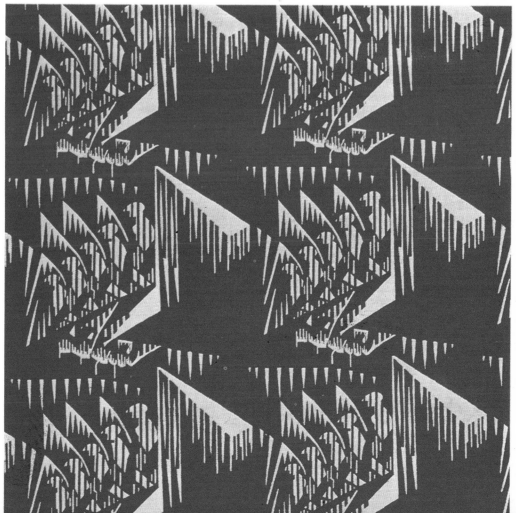

Decorative cotton print
1924-1925
Designed by O. Griun
The V. Mukhina Higher School of
Art and Design, Leningrad.

facing page:
"Mechanization of the Red Army"
Sateen
1933
Designed by L. Raitser
The I. Yasinskaya Collection,
Leningrad.

"The Village Consumers'
Cooperative Society"
Cotton print
Late 1920s
Designed by V. Maslov
Russian Museum, Leningrad
Acquired in 1931.

UNIDENTIFIED MILLS
from the Ivanovo collection

Decorative sateen
Early 1930s
Designed by S. Burylin (?)
Russian Museum, Leningrad
Acquired in 1931.

Decorative cotton print
Late 1920s-early 1930s
Designer unknown
Russian Museum, Leningrad
Acquired in 1931.

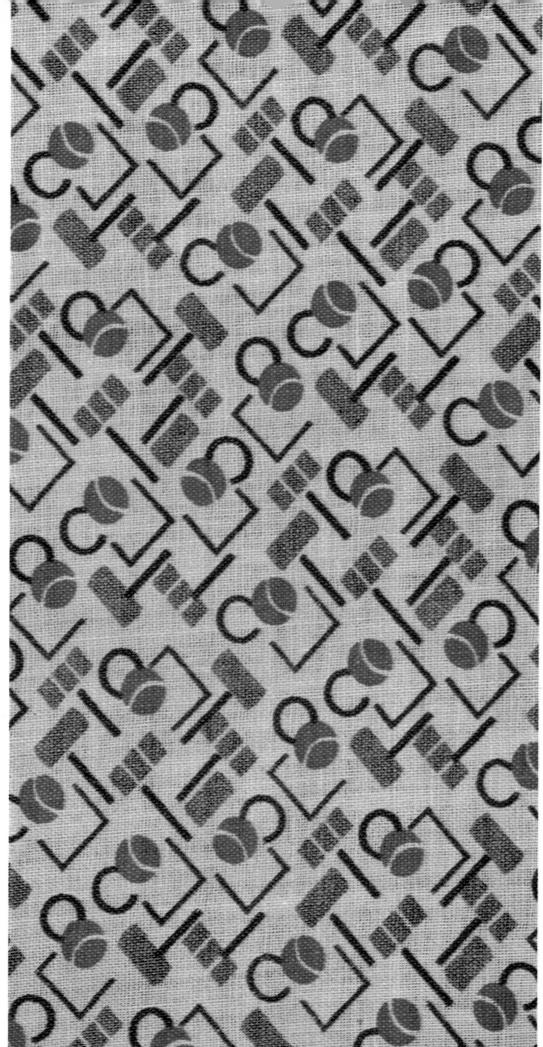

Cotton print
Late 1920s–early 1930s
Designer unknown
The I. Yasinskaya Collection,
Leningrad.

Decorative sateen
Late 1920s-early 1930s
Designer unknown
Russian Museum, Leningrad
Acquired in 1931.

facing page:
"Reaping Women"
Cotton print
Late 1920s-early 1930s
Designed by L. Silich
Russian Museum, Leningrad
Acquired in 1931.

Cotton print
Late 1920s-early 1930s
Designer unknown
The I. Yasinskaya Collection,
Leningrad.

Cotton print
Late 1920s-early 1930s
Designer unknown
Russian Museum, Leningrad
Acquired in 1931.

'March 8th (International Women's Day)"
Cotton print
Late 1920s-early 1930s
Designed by D. Preobrazhenskaya
Russian Museum, Leningrad
Acquired in 1931.

'Down with Illiteracy!"
Cotton print for the Soviet Republics of Central Asia
Late 1920s-early 1930s
Designer unknown
The I. Yasinskaya Collection, Leningrad.

Flannel
Mid 1920s-early 1930s
Designed by S. Burylin
Russian Museum, Leningrad
Acquired in 1931.

facing page:
"Airplanes"
Cotton print
Late 1920s-early 1930s
Fragment of a kerchief
Designed by O. Fedoseyeva
Russian Museum, Leningrad
Acquired in 1931.

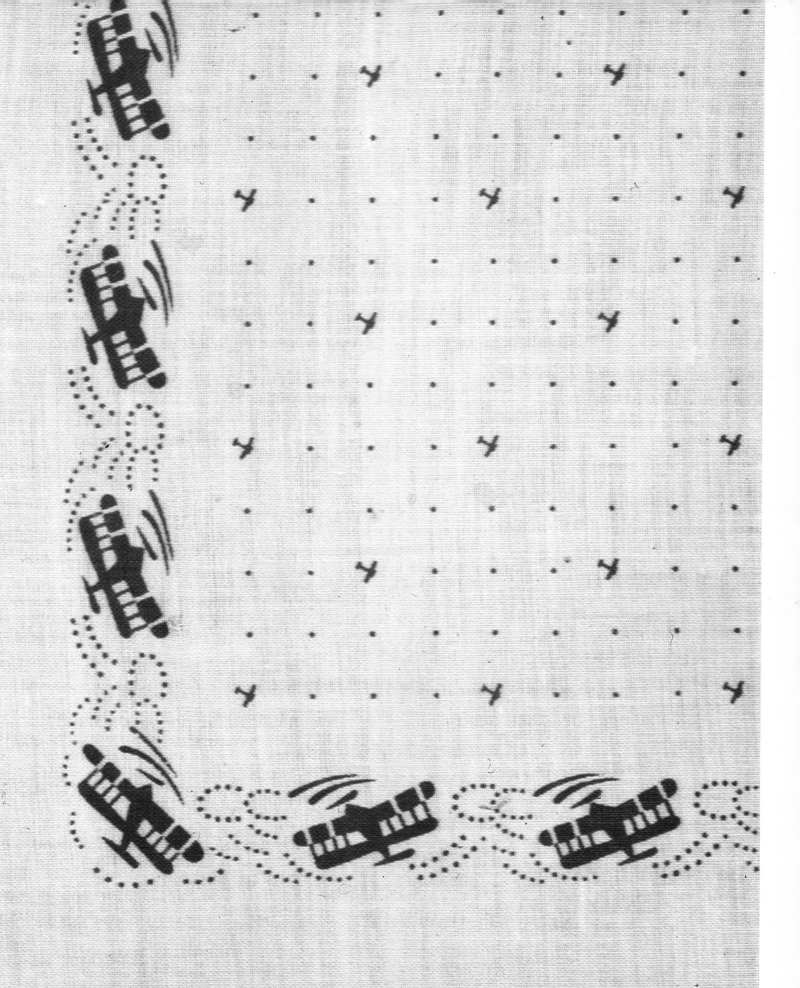

"MOPR" (International
Organization for Aid to
Champions of Revolution)
Serge
1929
Designed by D. Preobrazhenskaya
Russian Museum, Leningrad
Acquired in 1931.

Cotton print
Industrial motif
Late 1920s-early 1930s
Designed by S. Burylin
Russian Museum, Leningrad
Acquired in 1931.

Cotton print
Late 1920s-early 1930s
Designer unknown
The I. Yasinskaya Collection,
Leningrad.

71

Cotton print
Late 1920s-early 1930s
Designed by O. Fedoseyeva
Russian Museum, Leningrad.
Acquired in 1931.

UNIDENTIFIED MILLS

"Daily Life of the Peoples of the East"
Cotton print
Late 1920s-early 1930s
Designer unknown
The V. Mukhina Higher School of
Art and Design, Leningrad.

facing page:
Cotton print
Late 1920s-early 1930s
Designer unknown
Russian Museum, Leningrad
Acquired in 1931.

Cotton print
Late 1920s-early 1930s
Designed by M. Nazarevskaya
Russian Museum, Leningrad
Acquired in 1931.

Decorative sateen
Late 1920s-early 1930s
Designer unknown
Russian Museum, Leningrad
Acquired in 1931.

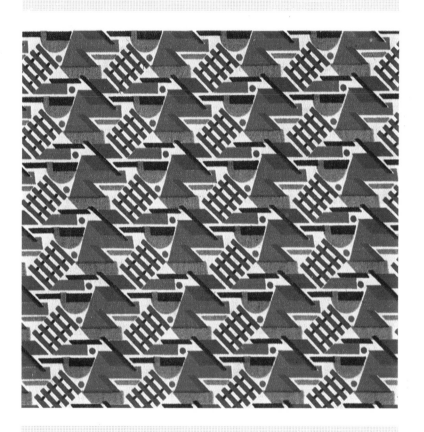

Decorative cotton print
Late 1920s-early 1930s
Designer unknown
Russian Museum, Leningrad
Acquired in 1931.

Cotton print
Late 1920s-early 1930s
Designer unknown
Russian Museum, Leningrad

facing page:
"Skaters"
Flannel
Late 1920s-early 1930s
Designed by D. Preobrazhenskaya
Russian Museum, Leningrad
Acquired in 1931.

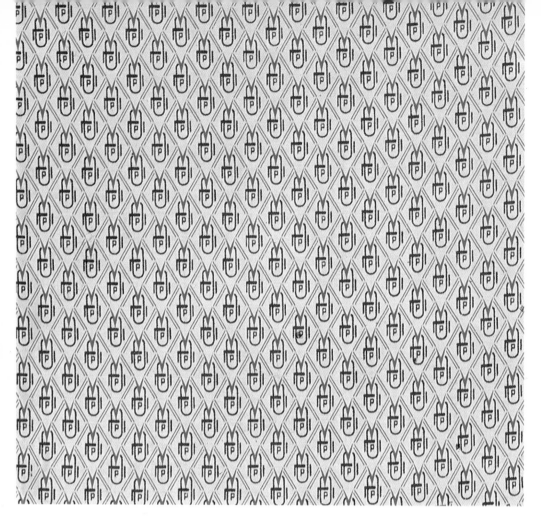

"MOPR"
(International
Organization for Aid to
Champions of Revolution)
Cotton print
1930
Designer unknown
Russian Museum, Leningrad
Acquired in 1931.

"Air Fleet"
Flannel
1930
Designed by M. Anufriyeva
Russian Museum, Leningrad
Acquired in 1931.

Flannel
Late 1920s-early 1930s
Designer unknown
Russian Museum, Leningrad
Acquired in 1931.

Armure
Late 1920s-early 1930s
Designer unknown
Russian Museum, Leningrad
Acquired in 1931.

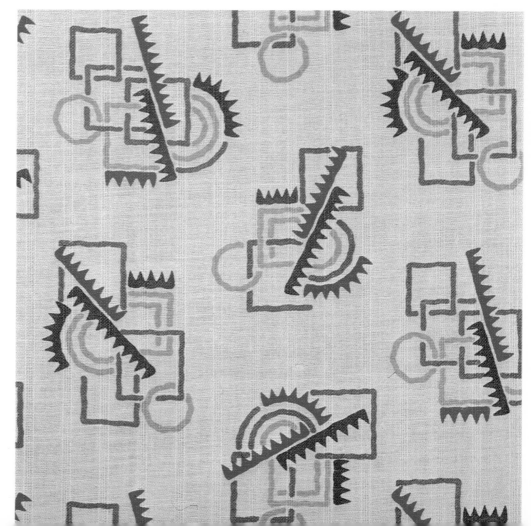

"Navy"
Sateen
Late 1920s-early 1930s
Designed by V. Lotonina
The V. Mukhina Higher School of
Art and Design, Leningrad.

facing page:
"Young Pioneers Marching"
Armure
Late 1920s-early 1930s
Designed by M. Khvostenko
Russian Museum, Leningrad
Acquired in 1931.

"Construction Site"
Cotton print
Late 1920s-1930s
Designed by F. Antonov
Russian Museum, Leningrad
Acquired in 1931.

Flannel
Late 1920s-early 1930s
Designer unknown
Russian Museum, Leningrad
Acquired in 1931.

Flannel
Late 1920s-early 1930s
Designer unknown
Russian Museum, Leningrad
Acquired in 1931.

Flannel
Late 1920s-early 1930s
Designer unknown
Russian Museum, Leningrad
Acquired in 1931.

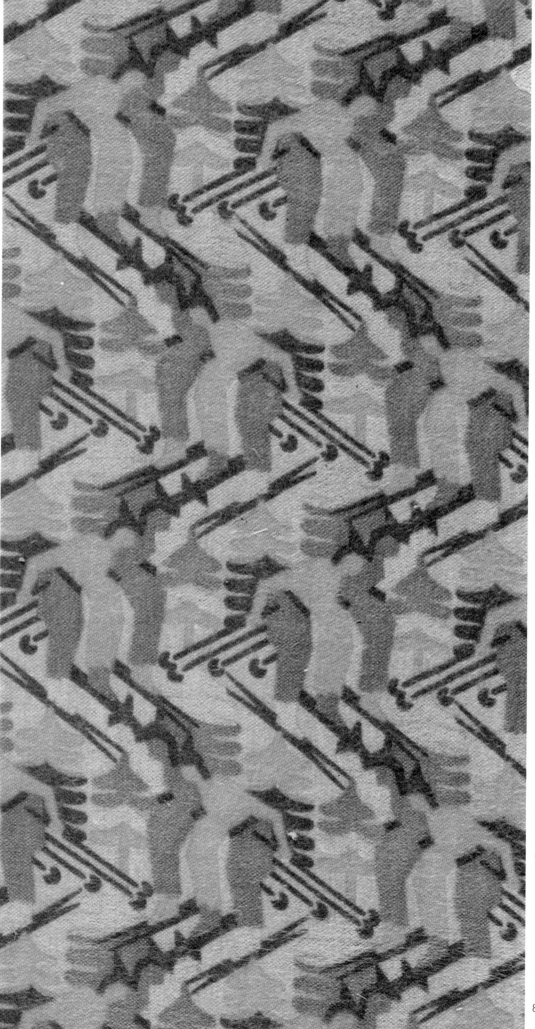

"Gathering Cotton"
Sateen
Early 1930s
Designed by M. Nazarevskaya
The I. Yasinskaya Collection,
Leningrad.

facing page:
"Hydroelectric Plant"
Flannel
Early 1930s
Designed by D. Preobrazhenskay
The I. Yasinskaya Collection,
Leningrad.

Flannel
Late 1920s-early 1930s
Designer unknown
Russian Museum, Leningrad
Acquired in 1931.

VERA SLUTSKAYA, PIOTR ALEXEYEV, Y. SVERDLOV
& FIRST COTTON-PRINTING MILLS

"The October Revolution"
Cotton print
1930
Designed by Belozemtseva
Russian Museum, Leningrad
Acquired in 1931.

facing page:
"Air Squadron"
Volta (a thin cotton fabric)
1929
Fragment of a kerchief
Designed by T. Chachkhiani
Russian Museum, Leningrad
Acquired in 1931.

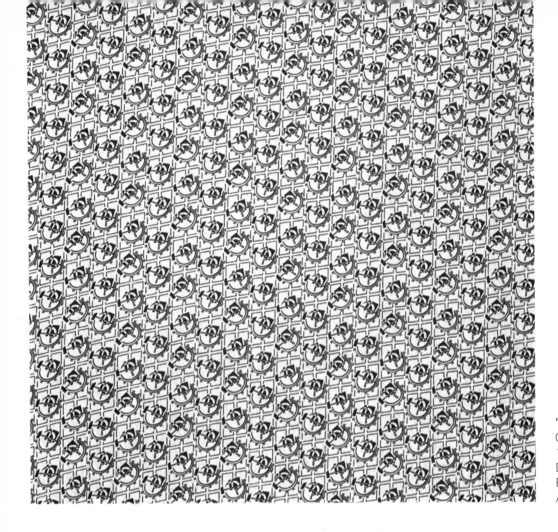

"Sickle, Hammer and Gear"
Cotton print
1930
Designer unknown
Russian Museum, Leningrad
Acquired in 1931.

"Spools"
Serge
1928
Designed by O. Griun
Russian Museum, Leningrad
Acquired in 1931.

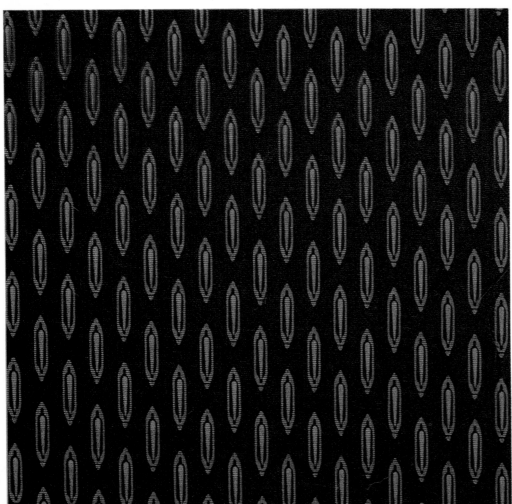

"The USSR"
Maya (a thin cotton fabric)
Late 1920s-early 1930s
Designer unknown
Russian Museum, Leningrad
Acquired in 1931.

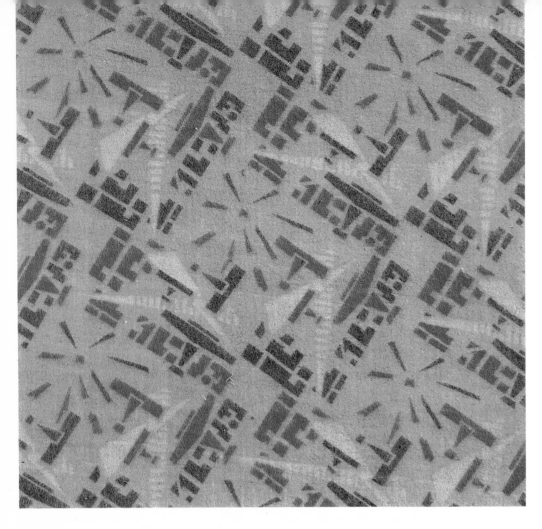

"Airplanes Flying"
Flannel
1930
Designer unknown
Russian Museum, Leningrad
Acquired in 1931.

"Tractor"
Flannel
1930
Designer unknown
Russian Museum, Leningrad
Acquired in 1931.

Volta
(a thin cotton fabric)
1929
Designed by E. Nikitina
Russian Museum, Leningrad
Acquired in 1931.

"Electrification of the Village"
Cotton print
1929
Fragment of a kerchief
Designer unknown
Russian Museum, Leningrad
Acquired in 1931.

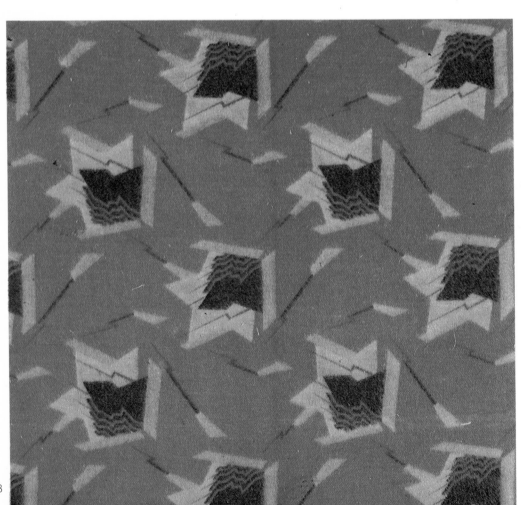

"Red Army Man on Guard"
Flannel
1930
Designed by E. Bykov
Russian Museum, Leningrad
Acquired in 1931.

5th OCTOBER, THIRD INTERNATIONAL,
"KRASNAYA TALKA", N. ZHIDELEV
& G. KOROLIOV MILLS

"The Turkestan-Siberia Railroad"
Cotton print
Early 1930s
Designer unknown
The I. Yasinskaya Collection,
Leningrad.

facing page:
"Aquatic Sports"
Cotton print
1930
Designed by M. Anufriyeva
Russian Museum, Leningrad
Acquired in 1931.

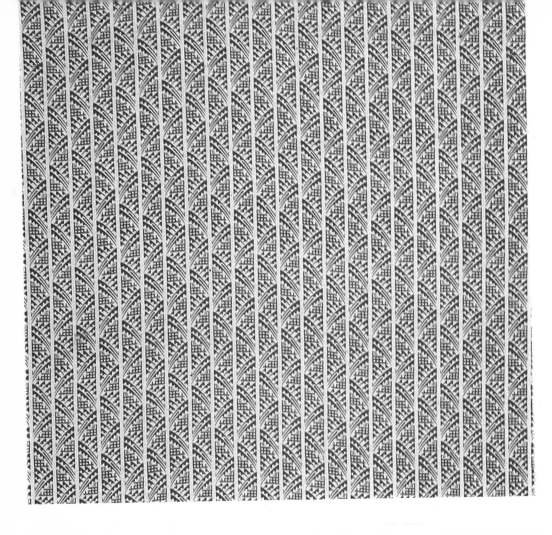

"Rye"
Cotton print
1930
Designed by Bobyshev
Russian Museum, Leningrad
Acquired in 1931.

"Seeding Machines"
Cotton print
1930
Designed by Bobyshev
Russian Museum, Leningrad
Acquired in 1931.

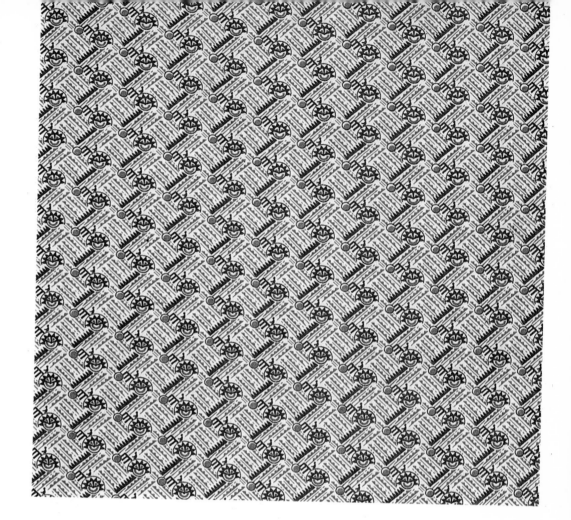

"Tractor"
Cotton print
Late 1920s-early 1930s
Designed by M. Anufriyeva
Russian Museum, Leningrad
Acquired in 1931.

"Young Pioneers' Attributes"
Serge
1929
Designed by Bychkov (?)
Russian Museum, Leningrad
Acquired in 1931.

"International Youth Day"
Cotton print
1929
Designed by M. Nazarevskaya
Russian Museum, Leningrad
Acquired in 1931.

"The Five-Year Plan in Four Years"
Armure
Late 1920s-early 1930s
Designed by Mityaev
Russian Museum, Leningrad
Acquired in 1931.

DATE DUE

APR 2 0 1986

DEMCO 38-297